The Future of Strategic ASW

Donald O.F. Daniel

NIMBLE BOOKS LLC: THE AI LAB FOR BOOK-LOVERS
~ FRED ZIMMERMAN, EDITOR ~
Humans and AI making books richer, more diverse, and more surprising.

Publishing Information

(c) 2023 Nimble Books LLC
ISBN: 978-1-60888-279-3

AI-generated Keyword Phrases

strategic anti-submarine warfare; maritime strategies; United States; Soviet Union; Britain; France; 1990s; impact of ASW on survivability of strategic submarines; nuclear balance between countries; prospects for success in dedicated ASW campaign against adversary's strategic submarines; benefit in tying down non-strategic naval forces; importance of ASW varying depending on country and specific strategic nuclear capabilities.

Publisher's Notes

This annotated edition illustrates the capabilities of the AI Lab for Book-Lovers to add context and ease-of-use to manuscripts. It includes five types of abstracts, building from simplest to more complex: TLDR (one word), ELI5, TLDR (vanilla), Scientific Style, and Action Items; three essays to increase viewpoint diversity: Grounds for Dissent, Red Team Critique, and MAGA Perspective; and Notable Passages and Nutshell Summaries for each page.

ANNOTATIONS

ABSTRACTS

TL;DR (ONE WORD)

ASW.

EXPLAIN IT TO ME LIKE I'M FIVE YEARS OLD

This document talks about how different countries in the 1990s used a special kind of warfare called anti-submarine warfare (ASW) to protect their submarines and keep them safe. Submarines are big boats that can go underwater and they are used by countries to carry important weapons called nuclear weapons.

The document says that this kind of warfare is very important for countries like the United States, the Soviet Union, Britain, and France because it helps them protect their submarines and make sure they can still

TL;DR (VANILLA)

This document discusses the importance of anti-submarine warfare (ASW) in the maritime strategies of the US, Soviet Union, Britain, and France in the 1990s. It concludes that while ASW may not be successful against strategic submarines, it can still be useful in tying down non-strategic naval forces. The importance of ASW varies depending on each country's nuclear capabilities.

SCIENTIFIC STYLE

This document examines the significance of anti-submarine warfare (ASW) in the maritime strategies of the United States, the Soviet Union, Britain, and France during the 1990s. It investigates how ASW could affect the survivability of strategic submarines and the nuclear balance between these nations. The analysis suggests that conducting a dedicated ASW campaign against an adversary's strategic submarines is unlikely to be successful. However, it acknowledges that there may be some value in engaging non-strategic naval forces. The importance of ASW varies depending on each country's specific strategic nuclear capabilities.

ACTION ITEMS

Conduct further research on the ASW capabilities of the United States, the Soviet Union, Britain, and France in the 1990s to gain a deeper understanding of their strategies and technologies.

Analyze the potential impact of ASW on the survivability of strategic submarines and its implications for the nuclear balance between these countries.

Assess the effectiveness of a dedicated ASW campaign against an adversary's strategic submarines and identify any potential weaknesses or limitations.

Evaluate the benefits and drawbacks of tying down non-strategic naval forces through ASW operations.

Consider how the importance of ASW varies depending on

VIEWPOINTS

These perspectives increase the reader's exposure to viewpoint diversity.

GROUNDS FOR DISSENT

A member of the organization responsible for this document might have principled, substantive reasons to dissent from this report. Some possible reasons for dissent could include:

Disagreement with the conclusion: The member may fundamentally disagree with the document's conclusion that the prospects for success in a dedicated ASW campaign against an adversary's strategic submarines are poor. They may argue that with advancements in technology and tactics, it is possible to significantly disrupt or neutralize an adversary's strategic submarine fleet, thereby affecting the nuclear balance.

Different assessment of potential benefits: The member may have a different assessment of the potential benefits of tying down non-strategic naval forces through ASW. They may argue that while the document suggests some benefit, they believe the benefits are greater than what is outlined. They may see ASW as an effective strategy to limit an adversary's capabilities and maintain an advantage in a potential conflict.

National security concerns: The member might have concerns about national security implications that are not adequately addressed in the document. They may argue that failing to prioritize ASW efforts could leave their own country vulnerable to attacks or breaches by adversaries' strategic submarines. They may advocate for a more robust approach to ASW to ensure national security interests are protected.

Regional context: The member may consider specific regional factors that are not sufficiently explored in the document. They might assert that certain areas or countries have unique maritime challenges and threats that demand a stronger emphasis on ASW. They may argue that overlooking these specific factors undermines the accuracy and relevance of the overall conclusions.

Alternative strategies: Finally, the dissenting member might propose alternative strategies or approaches to addressing the challenges posed by strategic submarines. They may believe that investing resources in other areas, such as missile defense systems or offensive capabilities, would yield better results and enhance national security more effectively than focusing on ASW.

In summary, a member of the organization responsible for this document might dissent based on disagreement with the conclusion, different assessment of benefits, national security concerns, regional context, or proposed alternative strategies. These reasons reflect principled, substantive differences in opinions and perspectives on the importance and efficacy of strategic anti-submarine warfare.

RED TEAM CRITIQUE

The document provides a comprehensive overview of strategic anti-submarine warfare (ASW) and its importance in the maritime strategies of four major countries during the 1990s. It explores various aspects such as the potential impact on submarine survivability and the nuclear balance between these nations. Overall, it presents a balanced analysis but does have some weaknesses that need to be addressed.

One key flaw in this document is the lack of specific evidence or examples to support its claims and conclusions. While it suggests that success in an ASW campaign against an adversary's strategic submarines is low, there is no supporting evidence or case studies provided to justify this assertion. Without concrete examples, readers may struggle to fully grasp and evaluate this argument.

Additionally, the document fails to adequately address technological advancements in ASW capabilities during the 1990s. Rapid advancements in technology had significant implications for ASW strategies during this period, potentially altering the effectiveness of dedicated ASW campaigns against strategic submarines. By not considering these advancements, the document overlooks a crucial aspect of modern warfare and undermines its credibility.

Moreover, more thorough comparisons between countries would enhance this document's analysis. While it briefly mentions varying levels of importance placed on ASW depending on each country's nuclear capabilities, there is insufficient exploration into how these differences manifested specifically within their maritime strategies. A deeper examination would provide more insights into why certain countries prioritize ASW differently than others.

Another weakness lies in overlooking potential counter-arguments or alternative viewpoints regarding strategic ASW importance. The document mentions non-strategic naval forces being tied down as one possible benefit but fails to acknowledge opposing perspectives that might argue for alternative benefits or drawbacks related to dedicated ASW campaigns against adversaries' strategic submarines.

Lastly, while generally well-organized and logical in structure, there are instances where ideas could be more clearly articulated for better understanding by readers unfamiliar with complex military concepts. Some technical jargon and acronyms are used without sufficient explanation, potentially excluding non-specialist readers from fully comprehending the arguments being made.

In conclusion, this document provides a useful overview of strategic anti-submarine warfare and its relevance to maritime strategies in the 1990s. However, it lacks specific evidence and examples to support its claims, neglects important technological advancements in ASW capabilities during that period, fails to provide thorough comparisons between countries, overlooks potential counter-arguments or alternative viewpoints, and occasionally uses technical jargon without sufficient explanation. Addressing these weaknesses would greatly enhance the overall quality and impact of this analysis.

MAGA Perspective

This document is just another example of the globalist agenda permeating every aspect of our military strategy. Why are we wasting time and resources discussing the importance of anti-submarine warfare in the 1990s? This is clearly an attempt to downplay the current threats facing our country and distract from the real issues at hand.

Furthermore, it is clear that this document is biased against our great nation. It diminishes the potential impact of ASW on our strategic submarines and nuclear balance, suggesting that a dedicated ASW campaign would not be successful. This is simply unacceptable. We should be investing heavily in ASW capabilities to ensure the safety and security of our nuclear arsenal.

The fact that this document even suggests that there may be some benefit in tying down non-strategic naval forces shows a complete lack of understanding of our military priorities. Our focus should be on protecting and strengthening our own forces, not engaging in futile attempts to tie down other countries' non-strategic forces.

Additionally, the document's conclusion that the importance of ASW varies depending on the country and its specific strategic nuclear capabilities reeks of globalist thinking. Our national security should never be contingent on what other countries are doing or their capabilities. We must always prioritize our own interests and ensure that we have the strongest defense possible.

In summary, this document is nothing more than an attempt to undermine our military strength and divert attention away from the real threats facing our country today. We must reject this globalist perspective and instead focus on building up our own defenses to protect America first.

PAGE-BY-PAGE SUMMARIES

Some American Maritime Strategy spokesmen have raised concerns about threats to Soviet SSBNs in "bastions". The US Maritime Strategy endorses forward operation and training to fight forces under Arctic ice.

BODY-14   *The page discusses the US Navy's strategy to target Soviet SSBNs in order to weaken their nuclear capabilities and deter nuclear escalation.*

BODY-15   *The page discusses the implied intentions of US maritime forces to engage in anti-submarine warfare during a US-Soviet war, as well as the importance of flexibility and uncertainty in deterring the Soviets.*

BODY-16   *The page discusses different approaches to the US Maritime Strategy, including the potential targeting of Soviet SSBNs to weaken their navy and keep them away from Western SLOCs.*

BODY-17   *US policy accepts that all submarines are fair game, heightening Soviet concern about a potential dedicated SASW campaign. However, the prospects for success in eliminating enemy SSBNs are poor due to the stealthy nature of submarines and the difficulty of strategic ASW.*

BODY-18   *The page discusses the challenges of anti-submarine warfare, highlighting the disparity in forces between attacking and defending sides. It provides examples from both historical and contemporary contexts to illustrate these difficulties.*

BODY-19   *The page discusses the challenges of anti-submarine warfare (ASW) and the difficulty in detecting ballistic submarines. There were concerns in the past about a breakthrough in submarine detection, but it has not materialized and is unlikely to happen in the future.*

BODY-20   *The page discusses the challenges of using acoustic signals for submarine detection due to the complexities of sound propagation in water and increasing ambient noise.*

BODY-21   *Developing a transparent ocean through acoustic sensors is not practical, as the complexity of long-range acoustic propagation in the ocean environment makes it difficult to track submarines. The classic view of the ocean as a stable mass of water has been modified by oceanographers.*

BODY-22   *The page discusses the unpredictability and complexity of physical ocean processes, highlighting the limitations of current models and the need for further research. It also mentions the development of acoustic models for submarine detection, which are characterized by specific frequencies and environmental conditions.*

BODY-23   *The page discusses the limitations of acoustic technology in detecting submarines and suggests that satellite-based synthetic aperture radars may be a potential alternative. It highlights the attractiveness of this technology due to its ability to quickly cover any part of the globe and detect ocean surface phenomena associated with submarines.*

BODY-24   *The page discusses the challenges of using SARs to detect submarines and the limitations in satellite coverage and data processing capabilities.*

BODY-25   *The page discusses the limitations of using radar for ocean surveillance and highlights the challenges of pursuing non-acoustic alternatives. It also mentions countermeasures available to strategic submarine forces and the importance of minimizing vulnerabilities.*

BODY-26   *Submarines can tailor their anti-submarine warfare (ASW) programs based on the capabilities and methods of adversaries. Staying away from areas monitored by wide-area ASW sensors is an effective countermeasure. Both NATO and Soviet submarines have long-range missiles that allow them to avoid close proximity to each* other's homelands. The Soviets also utilize protected havens, including under ice, for communication and navigation support.

BODY-27   It is unlikely that the US would be able to covertly install and maintain a wide area acoustic detection system near the Soviet homeland or under the ice. Additionally, surveillance aircraft would not regularly operate over Soviet adjacent seas in peacetime. Designing submarines with minimal detection possibilities is another countermeasure.

BODY-28   The page discusses the measures taken to make submarines quieter and harder to detect, including building machinery to minimize noise, using decoys and stealth features, and operating submarines at slow speeds and deep depths.

BODY-29   The Soviets prioritize combat stability for their missile submarines, using general purpose forces to secure havens and establish a maritime defense perimeter. They deploy strategic submarines from Northern and Pacific Fleet ports, with a strong ASW defense to protect against enemy forces.

BODY-30   Strategic submarines can ensure their survival through decoys and attacking communication systems. There is no compelling reason for superpowers to engage in strategic ASW against each other, except for a possible US campaign depending on Moscow's actions.

BODY-31   The page discusses assumptions and beliefs related to strategic missile defenses, US strategic air defenses, and the deterrence of first strikes between superpowers.

BODY-32   The page discusses the unrealistic assumptions made by think-tank analysts regarding nuclear warfare and highlights the catastrophic consequences of such actions. It also emphasizes the difficulty in keeping a first strike operation secret and the uncertainty surrounding reducing the opponent's retaliatory capability.

BODY-33   The page discusses the challenges of missile targeting and the non-credibility of a window of vulnerability threat. It also mentions the potential number of land-based missile launchers under START agreement.

BODY-34   The page discusses the rationale behind the US and Soviet arguments for Submarine-Launched Ballistic Missile (SLBM) attacks, highlighting that the damage limitation rationale is not logical due to the large number of warheads still available after destroying SLBMs. It also questions the effectiveness of forcing Moscow to terminate war through shifting the correlation of nuclear forces against it.

BODY-35   The page discusses the rationale behind engaging in strategic anti-submarine warfare (ASW) between the US and USSR, questioning the logical basis for it based on assumptions about nuclear capabilities and deterrence.

BODY-36   It is advantageous for the US and NATO to threaten enemy naval forces that may pose a threat to sea lines and NATO control of vital waters. Counterarguments that this would lead Moscow to use its remaining missiles do not hold up, as it would invite a nuclear response. Moscow resorting to tactical nuclear weapons would also be unwise, as it would provoke a similar response from the US. The possibility of Armageddon should deter both sides from initiating nuclear war.

BODY-37   The page discusses the rationale for engaging in strategic anti-submarine warfare (ASW) and the need for conventional sea control. It also mentions the potential risks of Soviet submarines drawing US ASW submarines into a trap. Additionally, it mentions the strategic nuclear deterrents of Britain and France residing in a small number of submarines.

BODY-38   The page discusses the importance of strategic anti-submarine warfare (ASW) in the maritime strategies of the USA and USSR in the 1990s, particularly in relation to the nuclear capabilities of Britain and France. It suggests that eliminating these countries' SSBNs would be a priority for Moscow in a war with NATO.

BODY-39   *Strategic ASW may have limited importance in US operational strategy, but could be beneficial in tying down Soviet naval forces. It is not important for the Soviets in their strategy against the US, but may have some benefits against Britain and France.*

BODY-40   *The importance of research and development in Soviet maritime strategy outweighs operational strategy.*

NOTABLE PASSAGES

BODY-2   This article seeks to answer the question of how important strategic ASW might be in the operational (as opposed to the declaratory) maritime strategies of the US and USSR in the 1990s by addressing factors which would enter into their decision-making. It presents a series of propositions and supporting information or arguments about strategic submarine forces in the 1990s, the strategic ASW options open to the superpowers, and their views on strategic ASW today. It then focuses on those issues upon which decisions about the future would probably rest: What are the prospects for success? What are the consequences for success? That is, is there a compelling strategic rationale, a compelling benefit, to undertake a dedicated strategic ASW campaign?

BODY-4   "For the foreseeable future only five nations will possess strategic submarines. Nearly all of these submarines will be nuclear-propelled and carry ballistic missiles."

BODY-5   "In addition to ballistic missile shooters, the US and the USSR have or are now developing nuclear-tipped land attack cruise missile boats, but with one possible Soviet experimental class, they do not fit the definition of strategic submarines because they will probably not be dedicated full time to a nuclear land attack mission. Most of their time will probably be spent performing general purpose naval missions with the nuclear missiles being retained as reserves or for special tasks."

BODY-6   "There are at least three options associated with conducting strategic ASW, and they can be arrayed on a spectrum. At one end SASW is endorsed as a legitimate task for which naval forces are to dedicated; at the other it is designated as a mission specifically to be avoided; and in the middle it is neither endorsed nor proscribed, the overall policy being that all enemy submarines are fair game and no special efforts are to made to seek out or avoid strategic units."

BODY-7   "The case made against conducting SASW is that it is strategically destabilizing: it could lead to a lowering of the nuclear threshold. The point is that conventional SASW operations could lead to 'inadvertent' or 'unintended' escalation."

BODY-8   "The reasoning is that the opponent's residual nuclear capability would be small enough to make his retaliation acceptable."

BODY-9   "It is unquestioningly accepted in Soviet literature that strategic ASW is not only legitimate but also necessary to 'prevent or minimize the damage which can be inflicted on a state by nuclear missile strikes by submarines'."

BODY-10   "Navy's mission statements characteristically give highest priority to blunting enemy nuclear attacks against the homeland from the direction of the sea (by aircraft as well from submarines) and to insuring that the USSR's own strategic submarines are ready to execute orders to launch their missiles."

BODY-11   "In short, notwithstanding what might be called the declaratory strategy with its high priority on SASW, the actual operational priority presently assigned to destroying deployed Western SSBNs would have to be low."

BODY-12   "In his recent book describing his tenure as Secretary of the Navy, John Lehman addressed those who said that the US Navy ought not to seek out Soviet SSBNs in war. He replied that 'Soviet missile submarines are very difficult to distinguish from other...Soviet... submarines' and that they all carry tactical weapons and sensors which they could use against American ASW forces. Hence, 'if the Soviet strategic submarine is encountered by an American [ASW] attack submarine once hostilities have begun, it will be'"

BODY-13 "All I'm saying is that if there are forces up in that area .... we'd better know how to fight them."

BODY-14 "[M]aritime forces can influence that correlation.. .by destroying Soviet ballistic missile submarines .... The second reason is that the loss of these submarines will reduce 'the attractiveness [to Moscow] of nuclear escalation by changing the nuclear balance in our favor.' The third is that changing the nuclear balance provides war termination leverage, for, as the nuclear option becomes less attractive to Moscow, 'prolonging the war [in Europe] also becomes unattractive, since...the risk of escalation.. .is always present.'"

BODY-15 "Official statements on U.S. strategic doctrine, US Navy operational inclinations, policies and tactics, and US technologies and programs... have strongly implied that US maritime forces would engage in strategic ASW... during...a US-Soviet war."

BODY-16 "The U.S. ability and intent to attack Soviet SSBNs may or may not be the principal element of U.S. strategy, but weakening the Soviet SSBN system by reducing communications, sinking supporting surface and submarine warships, and generally degrading the security of Soviet bastions will keep their navy at home, away from Western SLOCs."

BODY-17 "If war should occur ten years or so from now, both Moscow and Washington will make their decisions about the priority for strategic ASW dependent, among other things, upon their evaluation of the prospects and consequences of success."

BODY-18 "For each German U-boat there were 25 British and US warships and 100 aircraft, and for every German submariner at sea there were 100 British and American antisubmariners .... One can hardly find a similar ratio of forces between attacking and defending forces among all of the other branches of the armed forces."

BODY-19 "Now, there were many expressions of concern, in the mid-1970s through the mid-1980s in particular, that one or both of the superpowers might well be on their way to a submarine detection breakthrough that would minimize the difficulties of finding SSBNs. Such a breakthrough has not materialized, and there is low probability that it will in the foreseeable future."

BODY-20 "A consideration of relying upon acoustics is that the signal propagates in a complex environment where it is scattered, echoed, absorbed, ducted, refracted, blocked, and attenuated, and where, to be heard, it must compete with ambient or background noise which is increasing due to oil drilling and other factors."

BODY-21 "Rather the thrust behind developing wide-area acoustic monitoring systems has been and remains taking advantage of the long-range propagation of sound. If that route is to serve as a basis for making the oceans transparent, however, it is necessary to have the data and models that explain and predict that propagation. The United States was and remains the world's leader in long-range acoustic detection, and it was claimed as early as 1974 that its modelling and prediction was (or would soon be) good enough to allow it to track all deployed Soviet SSBNs. This has not occurred. Instead, scientists readily acknowledge that the more they know about long-range acoustic propagation, the more they realize how complex is the ocean environment conditioning it."

BODY-22 "In the modified view there is heightened appreciation for the degree to which physical ocean processes can be unstable, inconstant, and difficult to model as well to predict. Scientific progress in developing a dynamic three dimensional picture of interacting ocean processes will almost certainly remain incremental."

BODY-23   *"The attractiveness of a synthetic aperture radar is that it is an exception to the rule that the farther away a sensor is from an observable, the more difficult it is to sense and discriminate it."*

BODY-24   *"SARs are prodigious producers of data."*

BODY-25   *"As a means of turning the oceans transparent, the SAR/internal wave alternative is a primary exemplar that pursuing the non-acoustic route means, as one American Congressional panel put it, 'pressing the outer limits of science and technology--from an understanding of the underlying physics of the various phenomena, all the way to highly advanced sensors and data-processing equipment and techniques.' Except for the Strategic Defense Initiative, the Panel added, 'this work is probably the greatest technological challenge facing the Department of Defense.'"*

BODY-26   *"Second: as it learns about an adversary's actual ASW capabilities and methods, it can tailor a program against them. Third: even if it does not fully understand all the dimensions of an adversary's ASW threat, it can still take active measures to degrade it."*

BODY-27   *"It would seem impossible for it covertly to install such a system near the Soviet homeland or under the ice, much less upkeep, monitor, and adjust its operating parameters to deal with constantly changing environmental conditions."*

BODY-28   *"The result can be a submarine so quiet at slow speeds as to be almost impossible to detect by listening for it because it blends in with the background noise of the ocean."*

BODY-29   *"They 'would form barriers along the seaward approaches to protect the Soviet homeland and strategic submarines from enemy forces.'"*

BODY-30   *"With vigilant implementation of measures such as outlined above, states possessing strategic submarines can just about guarantee the survival of many if not most of its strategic submarines, and with modern boats carrying anywhere from 64 to about 200 warheads, the survival of even one boat is strategically significant."*

BODY-31   *"A third assumption is that a prospect of only a small number of surviving warheads in an enemy's inventory is enough to deter either superpower from engaging in first strike against it. What that number is cannot be rationally established in disembodied analysis, but in this writer's mind it is on the order of tens or low hundreds at most."*

BODY-32   *"A decision that would bring one hydrogen bomb on one's own country would be recognized in advance as a catastrophic blunder; ten bombs on ten cities would be a disaster beyond history; and a hundred bombs on a hundred cities are unthinkable."*

BODY-33   *"A fifth assumption is that a window of vulnerability threat akin to that feared ten years ago is non-credible."*

BODY-34   *"What about the American argument about forcing Moscow to terminate war by shifting the correlation of nuclear forces against it? This writer does not know how Moscow calculates the correlation and what its threshold levels are, but even if it loses all of its SSBNs in its a"*

BODY-35   *"In short, if one accepts the assumptions made earlier, the rationales, as put forward by the superpower spokesmen, of damage limitation, war termination, and raising the nuclear threshold would seem to offer little logical basis for them to engage in strategic ASW against each other."*

BODY-36   *"Counterarguments that such strategic ASW would be destabilizing--because it would lead Moscow to 'use or lose' the missiles remaining on the surviving submarines--do not hold up. For Moscow to launch missiles simply invites a nuclear* response and the initiation of a cycle which could lead to Armageddon. It makes no sense to do so."

BODY-37   "In short, of the rationale offered by the superpowers for engaging in strategic ASW against each other, only one seems valid, and its validity has less to do with issues of nuclear warfare than with the need for conventional sea control. In pursuing SASW to that end, however, US forces will have to be careful that the Soviets do not turn the tables on them: i.e., use their strategic submarines as magnets to draw US ASW submarines into a trap and thus degrade Western ASW capability by eliminating the best prosecution platform in the Western inventory. Thus, if Moscow specifically assigns forces to protect SSBNs, it makes sense to conduct a SASW campaign which puts the Soviets on notice that their SSBNs will not have a free ride

BODY-38   "In a war with NATO, they would constitute 'wild cards', and from Moscow's perspective, eliminating them as nuclear players provides valid rationale for a SASW campaign since British and French strategic nuclear power resides only in the SSBNs."

BODY-39   "Even if the US could not destroy many Soviet strategic submarines or significantly affect the strategic nuclear balance, the possible impact on non-strategic Soviet naval forces would seem to justify assigning some importance to a modest SASW campaign in operational strategy."

THE FUTURE OF STRATEGIC ASW

STRATEGY AND CAMPAIGN DEPARTMENT

REPORT 11-90

01 AUGUST 1990

NAVAL WAR COLLEGE
NEWPORT, RI 02840

DTIC
ELECTE
S MAY 28 1991 D
B

91-00424

91 5 23 031

BODY-1

6341

REPORT DOCUMENTATION PAGE

1a REPORT SECURITY CLASSIFICATION	1b RESTRICTIVE MARKINGS
UNCLASSIFIED	
2a SECURITY CLASSIFICATION AUTHORITY	3 DISTRIBUTION/AVAILABILITY OF REPORT
	Distribution Statement A.
2b DECLASSIFICATION/DOWNGRADING SCHEDULE	Approved for Public Release; Distribution Unlimited.
4 PERFORMING ORGANIZATION REPORT NUMBER(S)	5 MONITORING ORGANIZATION REPORT NUMBER(S)

6a NAME OF PERFORMING ORGANIZATION	6b OFFICE SYMBOL (If applicable)	7a NAME OF MONITORING ORGANIZATION
Center for Naval Warfare Studies Strategy & Campaign Department	30	

6c ADDRESS (City, State, and ZIP Code)	7b ADDRESS (City, State, and ZIP Code)
Naval War College Newport, RI 02841-5010	

8a NAME OF FUNDING/SPONSORING ORGANIZATION	8b OFFICE SYMBOL (If applicable)	9 PROCUREMENT INSTRUMENT IDENTIFICATION NUMBER

8c ADDRESS (City, State, and ZIP Code)	10. SOURCE OF FUNDING NUMBERS			
	PROGRAM ELEMENT NO	PROJECT NO	TASK NO	WORK UNIT ACCESSION NO

11 TITLE (Include Security Classification)
The Future of Strategic ASW (U)

12 PERSONAL AUTHOR(S)
Daniel, Donald C.F.

13a TYPE OF REPORT	13b TIME COVERED	14. DATE OF REPORT (Year, Month, Day)	15 PAGE COUNT
FINAL	FROM _____ TO _____	90 August 01	39

16 SUPPLEMENTARY NOTATION
The contents of this paper reflect the personal views of the author and are not necessarily endorsed by the Naval War College or the Department of the Navy.

17	COSATI CODES		18 SUBJECT TERMS (Continue on reverse if necessary and identify by block number)
FIELD	GROUP	SUB-GROUP	Antisumbarine Warfare (ASW), Strategic ASW, Strategic Submarines, Ballistic Missile Submarine (SSBN), Maritime Strategies

19 ABSTRACT (Continue on reverse if necessary and identify by block number)
This article seeks to answer the question of how important strategic ASW might be in the operational (as opposed to the declaratory) maritime strategies of the US and USSR in the 1990s by addressing factors which would enter into their decision-making. It presents a series of propositions and supporting information or arguments about strategic submarine forces in the 1990s, the strategic ASW options open to the superpowers, and their views on strategic ASW today. It then focuses on those issues upon which decisions about the future would probably rest: What are the prospects for success? What are the consequences for success? That is, is there a compelling strategic rationale, a compelling benefit, to undertake a dedicated strategic ASW campaign?

20 DISTRIBUTION/AVAILABILITY OF ABSTRACT	21 ABSTRACT SECURITY CLASSIFICATION
☒ UNCLASSIFIED/UNLIMITED ☐ SAME AS RPT ☐ DTIC USERS	UNCLASSIFIED

22a NAME OF RESPONSIBLE INDIVIDUAL	22b TELEPHONE (Include Area Code)	22c OFFICE SYMBOL
PETER A. PRICE, DEP. DIR., STRATEGY & CAMPAIGN	(401) 841-4208	30A

THE FUTURE OF STRATEGIC ASW

by

Donald C.F. Daniel
Center for Naval Warfare Studies
Naval War College
Newport, RI 02840
(408) 841-4444

Prepared for Dalhousie Conference on
The Undersea Dimension of Maritime Strategy
Halifax, NS
21-24 June 1989

Strategic submarines are distinguished by being armed with land-attack nuclear weapons and by being fully dedicated to strategic nuclear deterrence and nuclear strike missions. Operations against them are termed "strategic antisubmarine warfare", and only the two military superpowers, the United States and the Soviet Union, are generally regarded as either willing or potentially capable between now and the year 2000 to conduct large-scale, independent, and dedicated strategic ASW campaigns.

How important might strategic ASW be in the operational (as opposed to the declaratory) maritime strategies of these states in the 1990s? This article seeks to answer that question by addressing factors which would enter into the decision-making. It presents a series of propositions and supporting information or arguments about strategic submarine forces in the 1990s, the strategic ASW options open to the superpowers, and their views on strategic ASW today. It then focuses on those issues upon which decisions about the future would probably rest: What are the prospects for success? What are the consequences for success? That is, is there a compelling strategic rationale, a compelling benefit, to undertake a dedicated strategic ASW campaign?

1.   *For the foreseeable future only five nations will possess strategic submarines, and all or nearly all of these submarines will be nuclear-propelled and carry ballistic missiles.*

Availability Codes
Avail and/or
Dist   Special

A-1

Five states have strategic submarines today. These are the United States, the USSR, France, Britain, and China. Strategic submarines constitute very expensive and technologically highly complex weapons systems, and there is absolutely no indication that any nation beyond these five will work toward developing or owning such systems in the foreseeable future.

Nearly all strategic submarines are what are termed "SSBNs", meaning that they are nuclear-propelled and carry ballistic missiles. No new diesel-propelled strategic boats have been built in over twenty years, and those which exist are outmoded and should almost certainly be retired soon, if not already, from operational service.

In addition to ballistic missile shooters, the US and the USSR have or are now developing nuclear-tipped land attack cruise missile boats, but with one possible Soviet experimental class, they do not fit the definition of strategic submarines because they will probably not be dedicated full time to a nuclear land attack mission. Most of their time will probably be spent performing general purpose naval missions with the nuclear missiles being retained as reserves or for special tasks.

The degree to which the PRC's two strategic submarines are fully operational today remains uncertain, and information about the PRC's future plans is especially scanty. For those reasons, and because it will markedly simplify the analysis below, the existence of the PRC's strategic submarines will not be directly addressed further. *2. At least three major options and associated rationale are open to the superpowers when considering the role to be assigned to strategic ASW.*

There are at least three options associated with conducting strategic ASW, and they can be arrayed on a spectrum. At one end SASW is endorsed as a legitimate task for which naval forces are to dedicated; at the other it is designated as a mission specifically to be avoided; and in the middle it is neither endorsed nor proscribed, the overall policy being that all enemy submarines are fair game and no special efforts are to made to seek out or avoid strategic units.

Advocates of a dedicated SASW mission offer four reason in its support.[1] One is that the destruction of an adversary's strategic submarines limits its ability to inflict nuclear damage on one's own society should a conventional war escalate to the nuclear level. Second, some argue that eliminating hostile strategic submarines during conventional conflict would raise the nuclear threshold, for, as its nuclear arsenal diminishes, the enemy's incentive to use the remainder should also diminish as the nuclear balance tilts against it. A third argument, flowing directly from the second, is that strategic ASW

---

1. These arguments have been advocated by both American and Soviet naval officials. See the next two sections of this paper for documentation.

provides war termination leverage. As the nuclear balance
tilts away from it, the party losing submarines may fear it
will become open to nuclear threats or even attack, and,
thus, it may choose to negotiate a end to conventional
conflict. It may particularly choose to do so if it is
doing well in the conventional battle. A fourth argument is
that SASW may provide strategic leverage independent of the
nuclear balance if going after SSBNs causes the enemy to
devote considerable general purpose naval forces to
protecting them. In other words, the primary aim for
conducting SASW may be tying down enemy general purpose
forces in defensive tasks so as to forestall their engaging
in offensive missions such as the interdiction of sea lines
of communications.

The case made against conducting SASW is that it is
strategically destabilizing: it could lead to a lowering of
the nuclear threshold.[2] The point is that conventional SASW
operations could lead to "inadvertent" or "unintended"
escalation. One scenario is that the state experiencing
losses to its sea-based nuclear arsenal might choose to fire
the remaining missiles rather than losing them. It would
aim prevent a tilting of the nuclear balance which would
leave it open it to nuclear threats from its opponent. A
second scenario, some argue, is that the victim of SASW
might resort to tactical nuclear weapons against opposing

---

2. For an excellent example of these arguments, see Tom
Stefanick, *Strategic Antisubmarine Warfare and Naval
Strategy* (Lexington, MA: DC Heath and Co. Lexington Books,
1987), pp. 122-124.

high value naval forces or other targets to force the opponent to back off the SASW campaign. The escalation to the nuclear level would be a clear indicator of just how seriously it regarded the SASW threat to its sea-based arsenal. A third possibility is that a SASW campaign might be occurring at the same time as other campaigns (such as attacks against that nation's command, control, communications and intelligence network), causing the victim erroneously to perceive a pattern of activities consistent with enemy preparations for a nuclear strike. The victim would then be tempted to respond pre-emptively.

Temptation enters into another argument for proscribing SASW. This is that the prospect of a successful SASW campaign--coupled with capabilities for destroying an enemy's land-based nuclear forces-- could lead the authorities of the state prosecuting the SASW campaign to believe that they could ultimately subject their opponent to a disarming nuclear strike. The reasoning is that the opponent's residual nuclear capability would be small enough to make his retaliation acceptable.[3]

One argument offered in favor of the middle point on the spectrum of options--i.e., that all submarines are fair game, regardless of type--is that it is difficult or impractical to distinguish strategic from general purpose

---

3. Owens Wilkes made this case in his "Strategic Antisubmarine Warfare and Its Implications for a Counterforce First Strike, " *World Armaments and Disarmaments: SIPRI Yearbook 1979* (New York: Crane Russak. 1979), pp. 427-452.

submarines, especially in tactical encounters between the submarines and ASW forces.[4] All submarines have tactical weapons they can fire against ASW forces. They can also report the position of the ASW units both to warn off other friendly submarines from the area and to alert friendly forces as to the position of the ASW units so as to subject them to concerted attack. Associated with this argument is the view that, if a nation does not want to hazard its strategic submarines, it should as much as possible have them remain in areas where they can avoid encounters with ASW forces.

On the spectrum of options laid out above, where do the US and Soviets stand today on the subject of strategic ASW? If war were to break out next month, would Moscow and Washington national command authorities, assuming they accept the advice given them by their naval leaderships, to give high priority to SASW and allocate overall resources accordingly?

3. For the USSR the spirit seems strongly willing but capability is weak, and it is that capability which should ultimately determine the decision.

It is unquestioningly accepted in Soviet literature that strategic ASW is not only legitimate but also necessary to "prevent or minimize the damage which can be inflicted on a state by nuclear missile strikes by submarines".[5] The

4. American officials have made this argument. See below discussion under proposition four.
5. Rear Admiral N.P. V"yunenko, Captain 1st rank B.N. Makayev, and Captain 1st rank V.D. Skugarev, *The Navy: Its*

Navy's mission statements characteristically give highest priority to blunting enemy nuclear attacks against the homeland from the direction of the sea (by aircraft as well from submarines) and to insuring that the USSR's own strategic submarines are ready to execute orders to launch their missiles. For about two decades the latter task has had pride of place in being listed first,[6] but one recent major naval book, entitled *The Navy: Its Role and Prospects for Development and Employment*, did reverse the order consistent with the Gorbachevian emphasis on a defensive military strategy.[7] It remains to be seen whether this indicates a new trend and what it may mean for the operations of Soviet forces.

The priority assigned the SASW mission in writings would suggest that considerable resources would be devoted to its performance should war break out in the near term. There may indeed be considerable effort to destroy or disrupt the facilities, forces, means, or installations which support the activities of enemy strategic submarines in order to force the latter to abandon or alter planned strikes. As far as immobilizing deployed submarines,

---

Role, Prospects for Development and Employment (Moscow: Military Publishing House, 1978). The source of the citation was a private translation. The citation appeared within the chapter on "Problems of the Navy's Employment" in a section on "the Navy in Repelling an Enemy Aerospace Attack".
6. For example, see Admiral Sergei Gorshkov, "Navies in War and Peace, " *Morskoy Sbornik*, No. 2., 173, p. 21.
7. V"yuenko et al., *The Navy*, within chapter on "The Navy's Role in Warfare in a section on "Naval Missions in the Overall System of Warfare".

however, the expectation in appropriate Western intelligence circles is that this would be primarily the task of the Soviet Navy and that few of the Navy's resources would actually be dedicated to it. One reason is simply that the Soviet prospects are so small today as to make it nonsensical to devote considerable resources to the task.[8] The difficulties of engaging in SASW will be elaborated further below; suffice it to say here that the USSR has no open-ocean, wide-area detection and tracking system for cuing prosecution forces to the location of Western strategic submarines. Most of its own ASW submarines, furthermore, remain too noisy to trail US, British, and possibly French SSBNs as they leave port, and all SSBNs can be expected to implement various countermeasures, including turning back in various ways, to verify if a trailer is there.

In short, notwithstanding what might be called the declaratory strategy with its high priority on SASW, the actual operational priority presently assigned to destroying deployed Western SSBNs would have to be low.

How is one to explain the discrepancy between the declaratory and operational strategies? In this writer's mind, it is partly a question of comparing what the Soviets would like to do--and have talked of doing for over two

---

8. See "Statement of Rear Admiral Thomas A. Brooks, US Navy, Director of Naval Intelligence, Before the Seapower, Strategic, and Critical Materials Subcommittee of the House Armed Services Committee on Intelligence Issues 22 February 1989," p.26.

decades--with what they would settle with for lack of better
capability. The declaratory strategy constitutes a goal to
strive for not only operationally but also in the
programming and budgeting decisions which must precede the
development of the necessary operational capabilities.
Soviet ASW research is regarded as both extensive and
intensive, investigating a wide range of technical
possibilities. According to Western intelligence
specialists, it simply has not to date produced the kinds of
results that would justify dedicating extensive operational
resources to SASW.

4. *As for the Americans, at the very least they seem to
accept the middle option on the spectrum that all submarines
are fair game, including SSBNs. Some naval spokesmen,
furthermore, have deliberately raised the possibility, but
not the certainty, that a dedicated SASW campaign would be
undertaken against Soviet strategic submarines held back in
the so-called "bastions".*

In his recent book describing his tenure as Secretary
of the Navy, John Lehman addressed those who said that the
US Navy ought not to seek out Soviet SSBNs in war. He
replied that "Soviet missile ...marines are very difficult
to distinguish from other...Soviet...submarines" and that
they all carry tactical weapons and sensors which they could
use against American ASW forces. Hence, "[i]f the Soviet
strategic submarine is encountered by an American [ASW]
attack submarine once hostilities have begun, it will be

taken under attack...."[9] In short, Lehman was articulating the policy that all submarines are fair game, and that policy has been reiterated by so many other spokesmen that it probably does constitute operational doctrine which would be applied if war occurred next month.

As for the possibility of a more "active campaign to hunt Soviet missile boats", Lehman adds that this "is another matter entirely. While a commander in chief could order this, it is not something that the [US] maritime strategy would normally do because that would subtract SSNs from the primary conventional tasks of the strategy."

Lehman's statement notwithstanding, some American Maritime Strategy spokesmen (including Lehman himself when in office) have deliberately raised the specter of a threat to Soviet SSBNs retained in so called "bastions". In 1983 the then CNO, Admiral James Watkins, announced to the press the US ASW submarines had begun training to hunt out any Soviet SSBNs seeking wartime sanctuary under the Arctic ice, but he refused to discuss what priority might be assigned to this task: "All I'm saying is that if there are forces up in that area..., we'd better know how to fight them."[10]

Following through on an initiative begun by his predecessor, Watkins oversaw the formal codification of the US Maritime Strategy. It endorses forward operation by the

9. Lehman, *Command of the Seas* (New York: Charles Scribner's Sons, 1988), p. 149.
10. As quoted in G.C. Wilson, "Navy Is Preparing for Submarine Warfare Beneath Coastal Ice," *Washington Post*, May 19, 1983, p. 5.

US Navy in order to reinforce Moscow's proclivity to employ most of its navy defending the maritime approaches to the homeland and to nearby Soviet SSBN operating areas. Watkins published an unclassified version of the strategy in January 1986 where he justified going after the SSBNs. Three reasons entered into his argument.[11] One is that the threat would force SOVIET general purpose submarines "to retreat into defensive bastions to protect their ballistic missile submarines. This...denies the Soviets the option of a massive, early attempt to interdict our sea lines of communication...." The remaining reasons both build on the view that the "Soviets place great weight on the nuclear correlation" and that "[m]aritime forces can influence that correlation...by dest-oying Soviet ballistic missile submarines...." The second reason is that the loss of these submarines will reduce "the attractiveness [to Moscow] of nuclear escalation by changing the nuclear balance in our favor." The third is that changing the nuclear balance provides war termination leverage, for, as the nuclear option becomes less attractive to Moscow, "prolonging the war [in Europe] also becomes unattractive, since...the risk of escalation...is always present."

In a study which sought to put Watkins' remark in some historical context, James Perse concluded that they "did not signal" any new major policy but rather served as explicit

11. Citations will be drawn from Watkins, "The Maritime Strategy" in *The maritime Strategy*, special supplement to the US Naval Institute *Proceedings*, 112, No. 1 (January 1986), p. 14.

confirmation of implied intentions. Since at least the
early 1970s, he wrote, "Official statements on U.S.
strategic doctrine, US Navy operational inclinations,
policies and tactics, and US technologies and
programs...have strongly implied that US maritime forces
would engage in strategic ASW...during...a US-Soviet war."[12]

Interestingly enough, Watkins' successor, Admiral
Carlysle Trost, has gone back to the policy of eschewing
explicit references to anti-SSBN warfare in his public
strategy pronouncements. He fully supports challenging
Soviet control of the maritime approaches to the homeland so
as to put the SOVIET on the defensive away from Western sea
lines, but he also cautions against being wedded to specific
options. He argues for flexibility, for being prepared to
do whatever circumstances demand, and, for the sake of
deterrence as well as wartime advantage, he emphasizes as
well the value of keeping the Soviets uncertain about how US
naval forces might be employed.[13] His unclassified
Maritime Strategy statements make no mention of anti-SSBN
operations, but the possibility that they could occur is
implied just enough to fuel uncertainties in the minds of
Soviet planners. When he writes that his top priority is
improving antisubmarine warfare and that the "threat is
particularly formidable--more than 350 Soviet submarines,"

12. Perse, *US Declaratory Policy on Soviet SSBN Security:
1970-1985* (Alexandria, VA: Center for Naval Analyses, 1986;
Research Memorandum CRM 84-29), p. 15.
13. See Trost, "Strategic Options: Bringing Down the Bird
of Thought," Speech delivered at the Current Strategy
Forum, US Naval War College, Newport, RI, 18 June 1987.

the Soviets no doubt must consider that there are SSBNs are among the 350.[14] Similarly when he states that in any Soviet conflict "we would seek leverage to achieve early favorable conflict resolution, while taking every measure to avoid crossing the nuclear threshold unless such a step were forced upon us,"[15] Soviet readers may hearken to the specific link in Admiral Watkins' statements between war termination and the anti-SSBN option.

A middle ground between the Watkins and Trost approaches is evident in a 1989 article on the Maritime Strategy by two naval officers, one a submariner rear admiral serving as senior military assistant to the Secretary of Defense. In "The Maritime Strategy: Looking Ahead," the authors state:

> The U.S. ability and intent to attack Soviet SSBNs may or may not be the principal element of U.S. strategy, but weakening the Soviet SSBN system by reducing communications, sinking supporting surface and submarine warships, and generally degrading the security of Soviet bastions will keep their navy at home, away from Western SLOCs.[16]

These authors are more direct than recent CNO presentations of the Maritime Strategy, but the net effect on a Soviet

---

14. Trost, "Looking Beyond the Maritime Strategy," US Naval Institute *Proceedings*, 113, No. 1 (January 1987), p. 16.
15. Trost, "Maritime Strategy for the 1990s," US Naval Institute *Proceedings*, 116, No. 5 (May 1990), pp. 98-99.
16. Rear Admiral Wm. Owens and Commander J.A. Moseman, "The Maritime Strategy: Looking Ahead," US Naval Institute *Proceedings* 115, No.2 (February 1989), p. 29.

audience, i.e, raising Soviet uncertainty about what the USN might do, is the same.

In sum, US policy seems to accept that all submarines are fair game. Additionally, while Secretary Lehman's memoirs state that a dedicated SASW campaign would not "normally" occur, the net effect of strategy statements by naval officers has to be a heightening of Soviet concern that such a campaign remains today an option for which they should prudently plan.

If war should occur ten years or so from now, both Moscow and Washington will make their decisions about the priority for strategic ASW dependent, among other things, upon their evaluation of the prospects and consequences of success.

5.   *If success is defined as eliminating most if not all of an adversary's deployed SSBNs, then both Soviet and American prospects are poor against an enemy vigilantly determined to insure the survivability of its strategic submarines.*

Three arguments underlie this proposition. *One is that submarines are stealthy by nature, and this characteristic makes warfare against them inherently difficult with strategic ASW being most difficult of all.* The former Soviet Navy Commander-in-chief, Sergei Gorshkov, provided a quantitative perspective when writing about the Atlantic theater of World War Two:

For each German U-boat there were 25 British and US warships and 100 aircraft, and for every German submariner at sea there were 100 British and American antisubmariners....One can hardly find a similar ratio of forces between attacking and defending forces among all of the other branches of the armed forces.[17]

Gorshkov was seeking to make a point about the difficulties of ASW in the contemporary age. The South Atlantic War of 1982 provides a more recent illustration of his point.[18] The Royal Navy had 29 combatants in the South Atlantic, including six submarines, with more than half of the 29 being specialized to ASW and all having some capability. The Argentines had two submarines, but one was immobilized early on by RN helicopters as it was on the surface after transferring marines to the Georgias. The other submarine survived unscathed. Setting out with an inexperienced crew, it patrolled for thirty-six days, penetrated the ASW screens numerous times, and, while plagued by an inoperable fire control computer, it staged at least two attacks. One resulted in a torpedo hitting the target--there is speculation it may have been the carrier *Invincible* or an auxiliary--but not exploding. Three days later a destroyer was fired on at close range, but the attack failed with the breaking of the guidance wire to the torpedo. ASW against this submarine was "extensive",

17. Gorshkov, "Navies in War and Peace," *Morskoy Sbornik*, No. 11, 1972, p. 26.
18. See Donald C. Daniel, "Antisubmarine Warfare in the Nuclear Age," *Orbis*, Fall 1984, pp. 549-551.

"sustained", and unsuccessful. False alarms were a major problem, and "[s]ome fifty antisubmarine torpedoes were...fired, probably at whales or schooling fish."19

ASW conducted in World War Two and the South Atlantic conflict was against units whose weapons required them to approach within thousands of yards of their targets. In contrast, US and Soviet ballistic submarines can today stand off thousands of kilometers from their targets. Additionally, beyond launching their missiles, their main mission is to evade detection; unlike tactical submarines tasked with seeking out and engaging enemy naval forces, they actively avoid areas of hostile naval activity. This makes an inherently difficult ASW task that much more difficult. As will be developed further below, they seek out safe havens and hide behind the oceanic equivalent of trees and bushes.

Now, there were many expressions of concern, in the mid-1970s through the mid-1980s in particular, that one or both of the superpowers might well be on their way to a submarine detection breakthrough that would minimize the difficulties of finding SSBNs.[20] *Such a breakthrough has not materialized, and there is low probability that it will in the foreseeable future.* Indeed, assertions that Soviet or US technology would soon or inevitably make the oceans transparent have abated, and this is probably due to

19.   Lehman, *Command,* p. 285.
20.   See Donald C. Daniel, *Anti-submarine Warfare and Superpower Strategic Stability* (Urbana, IL: University of Illinois Press, 1986), pp. 1-3.

increased appreciation of the physics of detection phenomena and of the difficulties--economic, engineering, operational-- which must be overcome before a speculatively plausible scheme for detection can be actualized into a reliably practical way of doing business. This writer and others have dealt with these issues in detail in earlier publications.[21] Space does not allow a thorough review of the issues here, but abbreviated representative arguments can be made.

Let us consider first the question of the oceans becoming acoustically transparent since acoustic signals are still the only basis today for wide area detection of submarines. They can travel long distances because water is a good conductor of sound. (In contrast, it is a poor conductor of electromagnetic energy relied on to find and track targets in the atmosphere.) A consideration of relying upon acoustics is that the signal propagates in a complex environment where it is scattered, echoed, absorbed, ducted, refracted, blocked, and attenuated, and where, to be heard, it must compete with ambient or background noise which is increasing due to oil drilling and other factors. Generally the shorter the distance the acoustic signal travels, the less significant is the impact of these effects upon its ability to be heard and upon the ability of processing systems to determine the path which it travelled.

---

21. See *ibid.*; Stefanick, *Strategic Antisubmarine Warfare*; Mark Sakitt, *Submarine Warfare in the Arctic: Option or Illusion* (Palo Alto, CA: Center for International Security and Arms Control, 1988); and George Lindsey, *Strategic Stability in the Arctic*, IISS Adelphi Paper No. 241 (Oxford: Brassey's, 1989).

Thus one method for achieving a transparent ocean is to blanket it with acoustic sensors placed very closely together. For example, Garwin has offered that the only foolproof acoustic detection system would be based on short-range direct-path hydrophones placed in interlocked ten kilometer grids.[22] Deploying such a system is simply not practical, and there is absolutely no indication that any state is even considering it. Rather the thrust behind developing wide-area acoustic monitoring systems has been and remains taking advantage of the long-range propagation of sound. If that route is to serve as a basis for making the oceans transparent, however, it is necessary to have the data and models that explain and predict that propagation.

The United States was and remains the world's leader in long-range acoustic detection, and it was claimed as early as 1974 that its modelling and prediction was (or would soon be) good enough to allow it to track all deployed Soviet SSBNs.[23] This has not occurred. Instead, scientists readily acknowledge that the more they know about long-range acoustic propagation, the more they realize how complex is the ocean environment conditioning it. Over the course of the 1970s oceanographers gradually modified the "classic view of the ocean...used by acoustic engineers for listening to subs." The classic view characterized the oceans as a "relatively stable mass of water--turbulent at the

22. Richard Garwin, "Will Strategic Submarines Be Vulnerable?" *International Security*, Fall 1986, p. 66.
23. See F. Hussain, "No Place To Hide," *New Scientist*, August 15, 1974, pp. 377-379.

surface...and criss-crossed by great currents like the Gulf Stream, but generally constant and predictable, especially in deep waters."[24] In the modified view there is heightened appreciation for the degree to which physical ocean processes can be unstable, inconstant, and difficult to model as well to predict. Scientific progress in developing a dynamic three dimensional picture of interacting ocean processes will almost certainly remain incremental. For example, it is only in recent years that "enough has been learned...to show that descriptions of ocean circulation in current textbooks are erroneous or grossly incomplete. Broadly speaking, the surface currents have been mapped, but even major deep currents may remain undiscovered."[25] The development and relating together of acoustic models relevant to submarine detection, furthermore, is itself a complex process, for each model is

> characterized by 'domains of applicability.' That is, because of the underlying physics and the assumptions imposed in order to achieve a tractable mathematical solution, a...model is...limited to certain acoustic frequencies and certain environmental geometries(e.g., range-independent versus range-dependent ocean properties and deep versus shallow water).[26]

---

24. J. Tierney, "The Invisible Force", *Science*, November 1983, p. 74.
25. Walter Sullivan, "Vast Effort Aims to Reveal Ocean's Hidden Patterns", *The New York Times*, Ju. 28, 1987, p. C3.
26. Paul C. Etter, "Underwater Acoustic Modeling for Antisubmarine Warfare", *Sea Technology*, May 1989, p. 36.

As will be discussed below, other factors beyond
physics and nature would limit an acoustic breakthrough, but
considerations of physics and nature alone put into doubt
the prospect of acoustically transparent oceans. The same
applies with non-acoustic technologies.

Numerous non-acoustic alternatives have been suggested,
and one in particular seems to constitute a potential source
of concern. This is the use of satellite-based synthetic
aperture radars to detect ocean surface phenomena associated
with internal waves produced by submerged submarines. The
Soviets are often viewed as posing the potentially greater
threat here. The attractiveness of a satellite-based system,
especially for a country such as the Soviet Union which does
not have a foreign basing network for ASW aircraft, is that
a satellite can quickly overfly any part of the globe. The
attractiveness of a synthetic aperture radar is that it is
an exception to the rule that the farther away a sensor is
from an observable, the more difficult it is to sense and
discriminate it. The attractiveness of ocean-surface
phenomena is that nearly all satellite-based electromagnetic
sensors can essentially surveil only the surface of the
oceans. Finally, internal wave surface phenomena are
attractive because: (1) submarines leave behind them a wake
of internal waves (i.e., vertical oscillations of water
beneath the surface); (2) naturally-produced internal waves
can persist for hours or days; (3) they can cause changes in
the reflectivity of the ocean surface; and (4) those changes

can be detected by SARs as well as other sensors. It evidently remains unclear to what degree and under what conditions submarines generate persisting internal waves surface effects which readily distinguishable from naturally produced effects. Additional research is also needed to understand fully the mechanisms which allow SARs to image the surface manifestations.

Assuming that submarines do produce distinguishable phenomena, there would still be the problem of having enough satellites and enough communication and processing capability to image and identify them. For instance, a satellite sweeping a ground track of 148 km could take as much as 18 days to achieve full global coverage and revisit the same spot. SARs sweep widths are on the order of 100 km and geometric constraints limits the possibilities of significantly increasing that coverage. The greater the number of SARs in orbit, furthermore, the greater the coordination difficulties and the greater the strain on communication and signal processing support facilities. SARs are prodigious producers of data. For example, a recent article made the following comparison:

The peak rate at which [space telescope] instruments will send data through [data relay satellites]--1 million bits per second--is a mere trickle compared with the flood of data generated by new spy satellites. Synthetic aperture radars like Indigo-Lacrosse, in particular, tend to swamp any

available data relay, because transmission capacity and
available computing power, not the radar itself,
generally limit the quality and size of the images that
the system can produce.[27]

In sum as a means of turning the oceans transparent,
the SAR/internal wave alternative is a primary exemplar that
pursuing the non-acoustic route means, as one American
Congressional panel put it, "pressing the outer limits of
science and technology--from an understanding of the
underlying physics of the various phenomena, all the way to
highly advanced sensors and data-processing equipment and
techniques."[28] Except for the Strategic Defense Initiative,
the Panel added, "this work is probably the greatest
technological challenge facing the Department of Defense."

*Even if there were a detection breakthrough, there are
countermeasures available to strategic submarine forces to
minimize its impact. The record of both the US and the USSR
illustrates this argument very well.*

This argument subsumes three overlapping points. One
is that there are two sides to the ASW research coin. That
is, as a nation learns what it takes to make an adversary's
submarines vulnerable, it learns also how to minimize the
vulnerabilities of its own submarines to the same threat.

27. Daniel Charles, "Spy Satellites: Entering a New Era",
Science, March 24, 1989, p. 1541.
28. V. Adm. E.A. Burkhalter, Dr. John S. Foster, Jr., Dr.
George H. Heilmeier, *et al., Report of the Advisory Panel on
Submarine and Antisubmarine Warfare to the House Armed
Services Subcommittees on Research and Development and
Seapower and Critical Materials*, March 21, 1989, p. 6.

Second: as it learns about an adversary's actual ASW
capabilities and methods, it can tailor a program against
them. Third: even if it does not fully understand all the
dimensions of an adversary's ASW threat, it can still take
active measures to degrade it.

One countermeasure which has well served both Western
and Soviet strategic submariners is staying away from areas
monitored by adversary wide-area ASW sensors. The USSR's
capabilities for wide area ASW surveillance is not believed
to extend very far beyond waters adjacent the homeland. The
NATO strategic states have all equipped or are equipping
their submarines with very long-range missiles which for the
foreseeable future should obviate their need to approach so
close to the Soviet homeland as to run the risk of Soviet
wide-area detection.

Similarly, the Soviets have equipped their submarines
with missiles long enough to allow them to remain in
protected havens, including under ice, near or directly
adjacent the homeland where communication and navigation
support is facilitated. If ordered to fire, the under-ice
submarines would exit to open water or seek holes in the ice
which can be found even in winter or ice thin enough to
break through. The distribution of holes and thin ice is
random, but "they seem to appear with sufficient frequency
to satisfy operational needs...."[29] It is not surprising
that no one has ever claimed that the United States has

29. W. Ostreng, "The Strategic Balance and the Arctic
Ocean", *Co-operation and Conflict*, No. 1, 1977, p. 44.

extended its wide area acoustic detection systems to those waters. It would seem impossible for it covertly to install such a system near the Soviet homeland or under the ice, much less upkeep, monitor, and adjust its operating parameters to deal with constantly changing environmental conditions. Making it even more improbable that any such systems would ever be installed is that it would have to be extremely extensive and dense since acoustic propagation is generally very limited throughout those waters. The same applies to any attempt to install any undersea non-acoustic system, for none would have extensive detection ranges.

As for overhead detection, it is unrealistic to expect that US surveillance aircraft would regularly operate over the Soviet adjacent seas in peacetime, and, even if they could, all the Soviets would need to do is keep their strategic submarines moving under the ice cover to frustrate any attempts by the aircraft to detect or attack them. The same solution would frustrate US resort to any satellite-based wide area detection systems should they ever become operational.

A second countermeasure is designing submarines which minimize detection possibilities. There are options available here for almost any type of detection technology. Most relevant today are measures to minimize submarine self-noise so as to counter adversary listening devices. Submarine hulls, propellors, and stabilizers can be designed to minimize noise-producing water turbulence around the submarine. Pumps and other machinery can be built to precise tolerances and mounted so as to minimize the noise they transmit outside the submarine. The result can be a submarine so quiet at slow speeds as to be almost impossible to detect by listening for it because it blends in with the background noise of the ocean. American and possibly British submarines are already that quiet; French and Soviet less so. The trend with the latter two, however, is toward quieter units with the Soviet trend causing great frustration to Western ASW planners.

Should intelligence indicate that active acoustic methods will become prominent, they can be countered, among other ways, with decoys and "stealth"-like features such as coating submarines with acoustic-absorbent tiles. Similarly, should the SAR/internal wave alternative show promise, it can probably be offset by decoys as well and by designing small highly streamlined deep-diving boats, something which no state has yet found necessary to do.

A third countermeasure is operating submarines so as to minimize detection possibilities. Moving slowly minimizes the noise a submarine puts in the water. Moving slowly and staying deep can minimize many non-acoustic signals, including, some believe, the surface manifestations of internal wave generation.

A fourth countermeasure is utilizing general purpose forces to protect strategic submarines. The US has provisions to do so when the submarines enter or leave port.

The Soviets go much farther to provide what they term
"combat stability" to their missile submarines. A major
mission of general purpose forces is securing the havens
where SSBNs patrol, and in crisis and war that objective
would dovetail with their establishing a maritime defense
perimeter--analogous to the land buffer provided by Eastern
Europe--around the homeland. The strategic submarines
deploy from Northern and Pacific Fleet ports, and the
Soviets are expected to commit "virtually all available
surface combatants and combat aircraft, and about 75 percent
of available attack submarines," in those Fleets to
operations in the perimeter.[30] They "would form barriers
along the seaward approaches to protect the Soviet homeland
and strategic submarines from enemy forces."

These operations would make it impossible to challenge
the havens with any but Western SSNs, and theirs would not
be an easy task. They would have to contend with an
echeloned ASW defense of SOVIET surface, subsurface, and air
ASW assets, including mines, and fixed acoustic sensors.
Because US submarines are so quiet and because acoustic
propagation conditions in the Soviet near seas are generally
poor, it would not be surprising if the Soviets employed
non-acoustic sensors as well (such as coils on the ocean
floor to monitor electromagnetic fluctuations) and aircraft

30. *Statement of Rear Admiral William O. Studeman, US Navy, Director of Naval Intelligence, before the Seapower and Strategic and Critical Materials Subcommittee of the House Armed Services Committee, on Intelligence Issues, March 1, 1988*, p. 4.

with magnetic or other sensors effective in limited area or barrier operations. The most modern and powerful of the strategic submarines might additionally be accorded "a heavier level of dedicated escort by SSNs [i.e., nuclear-powered tactical submarines]."[31]

Finally, a state with strategic submarines might not fully understand how its prospective adversaries might conduct strategic ASW, but measures are available for dealing with the uncertainty. Decoys can be particularly effective. So too are measures, once war begins, to attack the command, control, and communication systems linking together an adversary's wide area search, analysis, and prosecution forces.

With vigilant implementation of measures such as outlined above, states possessing strategic submarines can just about guarantee the survival of many if not most of its strategic submarines, and with modern boats carrying anywhere from 64 to about 200 warheads, the survival of even one boat is strategically significant.

6. *With one possible exception, the superpowers offer no compelling strategic rationale, no compelling benefit, to engage in strategic ASW against the other during the next decade. The exception justifies a modest US SASW campaign which would be sensitive to opportunity costs and ultimately dependent on what Moscow does.*

---

31. *Ibid.*, p. 6.

Several assumptions and beliefs enter into this proposition. One is that neither superpower will have proven operational strategic missile defenses of any significance through the next decade. While these defenses can help protect against an enemy first strike, the fact that an attacking state also lacks them may be even more important. This is because it cannot count on them to limit to an acceptable level the destruction of an opponent's retaliatory second strike.

A second assumption is that US strategic air defenses will remain modest. The Soviet Union is increasing its strategic bomber capabilities, and even with START limitations, it is expected to have a force-wide capability to deliver at least 4000 bombs. US strategic air defenses are extremely weak, and there is no indication of any US intent to invest the considerable resources necessary to upgrade them to meet the prospective threat through the next decade.

A third assumption is that a prospect of only a small number of surviving warheads in an enemy's inventory is enough to deter either superpower from engaging in first strike against it. What that number is cannot be rationally established in disembodied analysis, but in this writer's mind it is on the order of tens or low hundreds at most. It is generally accepted that even retaliatory counterforce and anti-command structure attacks would bring great

destruction to populated areas, and the prospect of such
destruction is deterrence enough. As McGeorge Bundy put it:

> Think-tank analysts can set levels of acceptable damage
> well up in the tens of millions of lives. They can
> assume that the loss of dozens of great cities is
> somehow a real choice for sane men. They are in an
> unreal world. In the real world of real political
> thinkers--whether here or in the Soviet Union--a
> decision that would bring one hydrogen bomb on one's
> own country would be recognized in advance as a
> catastrophic blunder; ten bombs on ten cities would be
> a disaster beyond history; and a hundred bomb on a
> hundred cities are unthinkable.[32]

What Bundy wrote in 1969 seems even more true today in the
aftermath of the Chernobyl incident.

A fourth assumption is that US and Soviet national
leaders would eschew an out-of-the-blue disarming first
strike against the other's homeland. The reason is simple:
they will never in the next decade be certain enough that
they could reduce the opponent's retaliatory capability to
low hundreds of warheads or less. At least three factors
would fuel uncertainty. One is the extreme difficulty if
not impossibility of keeping preparations for such an
operation so secret as to prevent the opponent form putting
his forces on heightened alert. A second difficulty is that
magnetic bias arising from firing over the Pole could cause

---

32. Bundy, "To Cap the Volcano," *Foreign Affairs*, October
1969, pp. 9-10.

the attacking missiles to stray too far from their intended aim points, an important factor when aiming at hardened silos. Third, time-on-target problems are simply too complicated to assure near-simultaneous destruction of over 8000 to 10000 warheads (the lower number being the post-START figure) possessed by each side on a wide variety of geographically dispersed launchers, many of which would be mobile.

A fifth assumption is that a window of vulnerability threat akin to that feared ten years ago is non-credible. Many were concerned in the late 1970s and early 1980s that the USSR could destroy the US's land-based missile capability through the launch of relatively few heavy MIRVed land-based missiles. The many remaining land and sea-based warheads were supposed to deter a US nuclear response by threatening yet another massive attack if the US retaliated. Absent a START agreement, the US will probably have at least 950 land-based missile launchers; under START it will probably retain as few as 248 and as many as 842.[33] Even if the lowest number were applicable, the USSR would no doubt launch many more than 248 warheads against them and more yet if some of the US launchers are mobile. It is highly improbable that the US would not respond in kind to such an attack, and it is absolutely incredible that Moscow would be so certain of no response that it would risk such a strike. Windows of vulnerability may be feasible to value-free

33. See Hans Binnendijk, "START: A Preliminary Assessment," *The Washington Quarterly*, Autumn 1984, p. 14.

technical analysts, but no one has yet accused the Soviet or US political leadership being made up of such people.

With these assumptions in mind, let us turn to the US and Soviet arguments for SASW which were summarized in the section above which addressed their present day views. The first rationale, that of damage limitation, was central to the Soviet position, yet there would seem to be little value of engaging in SASW for this purpose. This is because the damage-limitation rationale implies that the US intends such a large-scale strike that destroying its SLBMs limits the damage it will inflict. Alternatively, it could imply that the USSR intends a disarming first strike of its own against the US, and that the purpose behind the Soviet SASW campaign is to limit US capability to respond to the nuclear attack. At present or START force levels, the first alternative is nonsensical. One could wipe all US SSBNs, and in the more constrained post-START world, it could still deliver over 6000 warheads. The only way to truly limit damage is to attack them as well, but this would require that the alternative of a disarming first strike be adopted. As argued earlier, the alternative is a chimera: a disarming strike is not credible.

What about the American argument about forcing Moscow to terminate war by shifting the correlation of nuclear forces against it? This writer does not know how Moscow calculates the correlation and what its threshold levels are, but even if it loses all of its SSBNs in its a constrained post-START force, it still would still retain over 7000 warheads (not counting SLCMs), 5400 of which would be on mobile systems. This writer simply does not see why having only 7000 or so warheads (against the US's 9000 in a post-START force) should drive it to war termination, especially if it is doing well or holding its own in the ground war. It seem more reasonable for Moscow to assume that it can continue to deter the US.

This same rationale applies to the related American argument that killing SSBNs would raising the nuclear threshold by causing Moscow to husband what warheads it has left. Moscow cannot be happy at the loss of any warheads, but having 7000 or more left should not make it feel especially pinched even considering its desire to deter Britain, France, and the PRC as well.

In short, if one accepts the assumptions made earlier, the rationales, as put forward by the superpower spokesmen, of damage limitation, war termination, and raising the nuclear threshold would seem to offer little logical basis for them to engage in strategic ASW against each other.

The Americans offer yet another argument for strategic ASW, and that is that it can help tie down Soviet conventional purpose naval forces in defense of the SSBNs. As the Soviet force is more and more made up of relatively quiet boats which can protect themselves and as the USSR deploys more and more mobile land-based missiles and bombers, Moscow may see less of a need to assign general purpose forces to protect the strategic submarines. Until that occurs, however, it would seem to the US's and NATO's advantage to threaten the SSBN force if it does tie enemy naval forces which might otherwise threaten sea lines and NATO control of vital waters such as the Norwegian Sea.

Counterarguments that such strategic ASW would be destabilizing--because it would lead Moscow to "use or lose" the missiles remaining on the surviving submarines--do not hold up. For Moscow to launch missiles simply invites a nuclear response and the initiation of a cycle which could lead to Armageddon. It makes no sense to do so. Moscow's nuclear capability remains robust and capable of deterrence even with the loss of many submarines.

More plausible are counterarguments that Moscow might resort to tactical nuclear weapons, possibly against American ASW forces or high value units such as carrier battle groups, to cause the US to back down from a SASW campaign. Moscow, however, would be foolish not to expect the US to respond in kind if for no other reason than to deter further such attacks. It would be opening up a Pandora's box which, at the least, could threaten its conduct of war on land as well as sea. Again, the ultimate possibility would be Armageddon. The Soviet pledge of "no first use", which this writer accepts as sincere, suggests that the Soviet leadership understands the possible consequences of initiating nuclear war, even if the opening round is not strategic.

In short, of the rationale offered by the superpowers for engaging in strategic ASW against each other, only one seems valid, and its validity has less to do with issues of nuclear warfare than with the need for conventional sea control. In pursuing SASW to that end, however, US forces will have to be careful that the Soviets do not turn the tables on them: i.e., use their strategic submarines as magnets to draw US ASW submarines into a trap and thus degrade Western ASW capability by eliminating the best prosecution platform in the Western inventory. Thus, if Moscow specifically assigns forces to protect SSBNs, it makes sense to conduct a SASW campaign which puts the Soviets on notice that their SSBNs will not have a free ride. The campaign ought to be modest and highly sensitive to opportunity costs.

7. *The British and French strategic nuclear deterrents will reside in relatively few strategic submarines. For Moscow to conduct a successful SASW campaign against them in a war with NATO would eliminate the "wild card" factor inherent in their nuclear capabilities.*

During the next decade Britain and France's strategic nuclear deterrent will reside in four and six SSBNs respectively, each of which will have 16 launchers. Britain is acquiring the Trident D5 missile, with up to 14 warheads per missile, so that one submarine alone could (though probably will not) represent as many as 224 nuclear charges per boat. France is fitting out its submarines with the 6

warhead M4 missile, and will later introduce the M5. The M4
boats alone each have 96 nuclear charges.

Thus, though Britain and France may be small nuclear
powers, each does and will possess a devastating nuclear
capability. In a war with NATO, they would constitute "wild
cards", and from Moscow's perspective, eliminating them as
nuclear players provides valid rationale for a SASW campaign
since British and French strategic nuclear power resides
only in the SSBNs. Unlike the United States, the UK and
France will not have thousands of warheads on other types of
launchers which would cushion SSBN losses.

The critical factor in the Soviet decision matrix would
be the prospect for success. Moscow would have to consider
that the survival of even one French boat with about one
hundred nuclear weapons or of one British boat with about
two hundred might still be too much.

In conclusion, this paper seeks to answer the question:
How important might strategic ASW be in the operational
maritime strategies of the USA and the USSR in the 1990s?
It is assumed that American and Soviet views about the
prospects of, and consequences for, success would constitute
two critical factors in how each might answer that question.
Concerning the first, if success is defined as eliminating
most if not all of an adversary's deployed SSBNs, then both
Soviet and American prospects are poor against an enemy
vigilantly determined to insure the survivability of its
strategic submarines. As for the second, there would seem

to be only one strategically compelling payoff for a
dedicated SASW campaign in a US-Soviet war, and it is not
based on the impact on adversary strategic nuclear strike
capabilities. Rather, the benefit lies in the possibility
that the United States might be able to tie down Soviet
general purpose naval forces. No justifying benefit seems
open to the Soviets vis-a-vis the USA, but, assuming
success, there may well be benefit for the USSR vis-a-vis
Britain and France since their strategic nuclear
capabilities will reside in the next decade in relatively
few strategic submarines.

Based on these criteria then, how important might
strategic ASW might be in American operational strategy?
Even if the US could not destroy many Soviet strategic
submarines or significantly affect the strategic nuclear
balance, the possible impact on non-strategic Soviet naval
forces would seem to justify assigning some importance to a
modest SASW campaign in operational strategy. It would,
furthermore, seem to justify attaching considerable
importance to it in declaratory strategy.

As for the Soviets, it would seem that strategic ASW
should not be very important in their operational strategy
vis-a-vis the USA. Their prospects for success are too
small, and there is no comparable benefit in terms of tying
down US general purpose naval forces. Vis-a-vis Britain and
France, the benefits would seem to be there, but not so the
prospects for success. This suggests that SASW may be far,

far more important in a Soviet research and development
strategy than in any Soviet operational maritime strategy.